SOARING THROUGH WINDS OF CHANGE

Seated With Christ and Equipped to Soar

Karen Harrison

PRAYER OF DEDICATION

May these writings go beyond the tapping of my fingers and a safety net, respirator, raft, or extended hands to gently capture the tears from a broken heart. May these words be a safe place of transformation for greater works.

Pen-writer of times, the one who captures more than the eyes and minds of readers, ignite a purpose in willing hearts to multiply and expand Your kingdom. I call forth those who might hide in these pages and are ready to be pulled by God's streams of unfailing love. His power of love blows "Fresh Winds" reaching the depth of pain with a calm rest of freedom. May the power of Your Spirit magnetize this book to draw the person in need of answers, wisdom, and comfort to change the course of their life. Oh Lord, let the winds of change breathe on us! Let a passerby join in the journey of hope and we will soar together by riding on the rafts of "Fresh Winds."

Isaiah 40:31 NIV-...*but those who hope in the Lord will renew their strength. They will soar on wings like eagles; they will run and not grow weary; they will walk and not be faint.*

Contents

INTRODUCTION

This 31-day devotional has four sections that include a scripture focus, stories, prayer, and space for reflections from the reader to jot down meaningful notes related to the meditation.

These shared stories are from life experiences along with my secret place of prayers which I hope will bless you. The reflection section challenges the reader to dig deeper in answering some questions from a personal perspective, which transforms these devotions into your personal time with God.

Having this book in your possession will provide answers you may be still seeking for or it will be a guide to develop a closer walk with the Lord. My prayer is that your heart and mind is ready to go higher and willing to break any barriers as you understand how daily living fits in with the truth of God's word. If there is a need to repeat a section, feel free to do so because the remaining pages will be waiting for you, just like our faithful Father.

INSTRUCTIONS

Habitually ask God for understanding before you read this book. Acknowledge Him as your guide and teacher.

Focus on the word of God. He wants you to understand what He meant, not what you think. Ponder over the written word of God until you remember it from day to day.

While reading the stories **identify common challenges or experiences** in the book that you have faced or has caught your attention for preparation. Remember you are not alone in any struggle.

Pray the daily prayers aloud if possible. Focus on the areas that convict your heart. God is ready to help. I have purposely been transparent to partner with you in the liberty of Christ in hope that you will experience His presence.

DAY 1

Praise the Lord, my soul. Lord my God, you are very great; you are clothed with splendor and majesty. The Lord wraps himself in light as with a garment; he stretches out the heavens like a tent and lays the beams of his upper chambers on their waters. He makes the clouds his chariot and rides on the wings of the wind. He makes winds his messengers, flames of fire his servants.

Psalm 104:1-4 NIV

FRESH WINDS

God's power exceeds what we consider untouchable such as the clouds. The movement of God is expressed in the above scripture relating to things that can be touched or perceived, like a tent, a garment, and servants. It is also demonstrated by the elements of the earth, like clouds, winds, and flames of fire. The discovery of who God is, includes his greatness, character, and His power that can transform a moment or a lifetime. Stop for a moment and acknowledge who is in control! *Be still and know that I am God....* **Psalm 46:10NIV**

MY SECRET PLACE

Today, my search to know you, Lord, is real to me. You have secretly waited for my need to ask for Your help. How silly of me to sit in an empty space and think I'm all alone. The clutter of my mind squeezes me into a place of loneliness. How can I deny Your presence and Your mercy that often stopped the plans that would have devoured me? It

8

is time to lift my head and stretch my arms in surrender to the one who has always loved me. You held back the penalty for my sin, which I truly deserve and kept me in sync with Your will on the borders of high tides. **Romans 3:23** says, "For all have sinned and come short of God's glory." Therefore, may the words of your infinite love leap up to my heart with the hope that my tenacity of faith will lead me to your true will.

PRAY WITH ME

Dear Lord, thank You for revealing Your greatness in my brokenness and carrying me through storms and into Your presence. I agree with Your word. *"My sacrifice, O God, is a broken spirit; a broken and contrite heart you, God, will not despise."* - **Psalm 51:17 NIV** Just when life appeared to be a total breakdown, You broke through! Breathe the fresh winds of life over me and shift the shadows of regret and hurt as I take a breath of Your hope and love. As I enter a brand-new day help me to think according to Your plans. Hear my voice echoing the psalmist, *"When anxiety was great within me, your consolation brought me joy."* - **Psalm 94;17 NIV** Your plans that existed before time are sufficient. Restore what is broken and decayed for the use of Your kingdom. Today, my search is to uncover the things hidden from my eyes and to gain an understanding of Your ways. Thank you for not giving up on me, as I have often done, and You waited when I didn't want to. Your love is more than what man can offer. Today, in Jesus' name I declare fresh winds of love and restoration are coming with power to enable me to be just who You said I am.

REFLECTIONS

In your search for truth, what have you discovered about God and yourself? Write down your thoughts as you read or pray.

_____

_____

_____

_____

_____

_____

_____

_____

_____

_____

_____

_____

_____

_____

DAY 2

I praise you because I am fearfully and wonderfully made; your works are wonderful; I know that full well.

Psalm 139:14 NIV

THE MISSING PIECE

The Psalmist recognized the creativity of God, and he reverently adored the wonders of His works. He realized the strategic plan of God in creating man and the potential when man implements God's plan. Have you ever tried putting a puzzle together and when all the pieces are in place you find an empty space that messes up the whole picture? To top it off there are no pieces left! Nothing else will fit in that space. You can't take it back to the store. A thousand pieces and one-piece messes everything up! The maker of the puzzle designed it with specific details and shapes that cannot be replaced. We are pieces with unique shapes, colors, and purposes. As with a puzzle, our feelings can lead us to believe that we have been misplaced and lost. However, God's canvas is never complete without you. For us to live intentionally, we must remain in God's hands and think like the Creator of heaven and earth. **Philippians 2:5 NIV** – *"In your relationships with one another, have the same mindset as Christ Jesus."* Then the question is always at hand, is He the missing piece? If so, that's an easy find, for He's too big to miss and He holds a place in His hands for you.

PRAY WITH ME

11

Savior, lover of my soul! What a humble awakening to realize my own weaknesses. Your word says ... *"My grace is sufficient for you, for my power is perfected in my weakness."*- **2 Corinthians 12:9 NIV** Your statue is my castle, my fortress, and although the sands of life shift with the seas I find safety in You. Nothing can take Your place or keep me from Your love, even if it's only in Your footprints. True strength is found in grace that reaches beyond my measure! With unfailing hands Your love has carried and held me up. Thank you for showing me a better way when I have often strayed. You became my lifeline and rescued me. I want my eyes opened so I can understand the times and seasons. Make Your ways more visible and attainable while I am in Your hands.

I am asking You, for Your kingdom's sake, to pull on those whose hearts are ready to surrender so that such deep love can be embraced. By Your grace my faith will produce the works of Your glory and destroy the works of darkness. I agree with Your word that *"As the body without the spirit is dead, so faith without deeds is dead."*- **James 2:26 NIV** May I become Your mouthpiece to warn others not to miss the invitation to a sustaining life. Today, my heart is surrendered and fastened to You, although my mind has often run ahead. Now love, power, and self-discipline will lead me to Your wisdom. Strengthen my stance and guide my steps as I follow Your plans. Thank you, Lord for another chance to keep in step with You! Thank you, Jesus! Scripture Ref.: **Jeremiah 29:11-13**

REFLECTIONS

In your search for truth, what have you discovered about God and yourself? Write down your thoughts as you read or pray.

_____

_____

_____

_____

_____

_____

_____

_____

_____

_____

_____

_____

_____

_____

DAY 3

Every valley shall be raised up, every mountain and hill made low; the rough ground shall become level, the rugged places a plain. 25- "To whom will you compare me? Or who is my equal?" says the Holy One.

Isaiah 40:3-4, 25 NIV

A COMEBACK

The writings of Prophet Isaiah express the power of God by using nature, which man cannot physically move and always refers to Him who is bigger than the things we cannot handle.

The above writings of Prophet Isaiah demonstrate the power of God using nature, which man cannot control. They also refer to His power, which is bigger than anything we can grasp. As with Israel, there's an echoing call in our wilderness of difficult places, challenges, and hardened hearts that can lead to destruction. A shattered state is one in which obstacles are both high enough to block our view and deep enough to create the illusion that there is no end to the darkness. The word of God says in **Romans 1:17b NIV** - *"The righteous will live by faith."* There is an urgent need to hear God's voice because faith by sight will always challenge our walk.

A word of hope is desired, but it must come from a holy place to rescue us from blindness and captivity. **2 Timothy 1:9 NIV**- says *"He has saved us and called us to a holy life— not because of anything we have done but because of His own purpose and* *grace"* ... Christ came to set captives free, bringing abundant life, and hope to a broken world. Can you hear Him calling through the high mountains of your life? You know, the obstacles that stand in your way. He sees them as ant hills. Throughout the seasons and times, various measures have been taken to help us comprehend what God is saying. His light gives vision in darkness and His truth shatters invisible chains.

Take a moment to slow down, step up, or step away from the chaos. He will clear the way as you listen. What seemed to be a setback was really a chance for a comeback. Are you ready?

MY SECRET PLACE

In the past I have been in a dark place and wandered around many times bumping into unwanted things, including myself. Oh, this sinful nature I despise, and only by grace can I sin less! Creation can never be greater than its creator; therefore, He rules over all even when it appears not to be righteous. Remember, everything God created at the beginning was called "good." It is a fatal decision to not trust Him in our daily walk because alternate paths look good but lead to major downfalls

Over and over grace opened the window to a new day, a shift in our spirits, a renewing of mind, and a coming home. He removed the blinding glare, allowing us to see the cause of the casualty. Now it's time to be renewed, restored, and revived by His grace to fulfill His plans. His mind has not changed regarding the life of his people. We changed! The word of God says, *"Jesus Christ is the same yesterday today and forever."* **Hebrews 13:8 NIV**

We must be willing to let Him remold and remake us, restore, and revive us! As a reminder of the required intimacy with God, a heart monitor's display reflects a heartbeat's movement in lines moving up and down. Like life's activities,

15

this involves crossing hills and valleys. There is no doubt in our minds that it was God who carried us through. Without Christ, what will I or have I achieved? Absolutely nothing! **1Corinthians 15:10 NIV**-*But by the grace of God I am what I am, and his grace was not without effect."* ...

PRAY WITH ME

Your light has shone even in the tiniest creases of my soul, hidden away from the eyes of the world. The Great Physician, healer of my soul, body, and mind. You cause my heart to be in sync with the rhythm of life. Remove the floaters from my eyes that often lead me away from truth and let my heart be at rest. Cause me to look past alarming sights and to see the hope You have clearly made known in Christ. There are no breakdowns in Your existence and Your sufficient grace will carry me through as I stay in fellowship with You.

You are the potter, and I am the clay. I am willing to be still as You rearrange my destiny. You instructed me not to rely on my own understanding, yet I did, so it must be altered. What a peace to know that You are all-knowing in all things. There are no secrets hidden from You. I am ready to catch the porton in my race of destiny by faith. Thank You for the comeback that leads to truth!

REFLECTIONS

In your search for truth, what have you discovered about God and yourself? Write down your thoughts as you read or pray.

_____

_____

_____

_____

_____

_____

_____

_____

_____

_____

_____

_____

_____

_____

_____

DAY 4

I call on the Lord in my distress, and he answers me.

Psalm 120:1 NIV

And everyone who calls on the name of the Lord will be saved.

Acts 2:21

HELP IS HERE!!

The cry for help is not a selfish cry to be saved on a dreadful day, but a cry for restoration to the newness of life. While looking for support and seeking answers, frustration and disappointment can quickly set in when people realize that their current course was a wrong choice and time is short. However, when we reach the end of our rope, which is really the end of our own will and way, help is available. The readiness to surrender results in a surge of renewed strength from a loving Father. The past cannot be erased, nor can time be regained from situations, but our past can become a tool of wisdom and understanding.

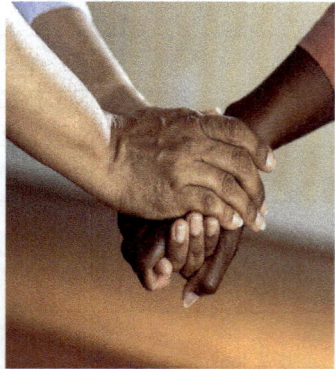

Have you ever met someone who is sarcastically called a "know-it-all?" Well, knowing someone who knows all things is beneficial. It is not about asking questions but admitting that you don't have the answers or even understand the process. The choice to be humble can open doors to receiving gracious answers.

PRAY WITH ME

Father, thank you for your grace and mercy. Forgive me for trying to manage my life on my own without the one who gave it to me. Throughout this process, I surrender my all to you, Lord, and ask that you remind me that I must trust you with this decision. **Proverbs 3:5 NIV**- *"Trust in the Lord with all your heart and lean not on your own understanding;"* ...

This time Your grace shall make a difference, and not because of anything I have done. Instead, I am willing to embrace Your dominion, power, and glory, and accept Your answer. My own ways have been interrupted by Your will, way, and presence. **Lord, your realness and strength cannot and will not be depleted or defeated when things don't happen my way.** You are bigger than my thoughts or hands, so I will follow Your lead, be who You say I am, and do what You ask of me. I surrender my thoughts to Your victorious power.

My present state and my future lie hidden in the shadows of the Almighty. There I rejoice, and I am glad. His victory has become mine, and I declare it to have been a fixed fight, paid for on a cross, rather than under the table. I am ready to carry the cross of victory. He is the undefeated champion of my salvation, and I will trust Him in all things.

REFLECTIONS

In your search for truth, what have you discovered about God and yourself? Write down your thoughts as you read or pray.

_____

_____

_____

_____

_____

_____

_____

_____

_____

_____

_____

_____

_____

_____

_____

_____

DAY 5

Blessed are those who find wisdom, those who gain understanding...

Proverbs 3:13, NIV

The beginning of wisdom is this: Get wisdom. Though it cost all you have, get understanding.

4:7

Whoever is patient has great understanding, but one who is quick-tempered displays folly.

14:29

COMPREHENSION AT ITS BEST

The word of God speaks about the need for wisdom and its starting point. To ask God for wisdom is to understand how to live God's way, rather than just cleverly using the deceitful wisdom of this world. With the Lord, this request may be different, but it is not out of bounds. God's word also points to the Spirit of wisdom that enlightens and empowers our minds to see and understand His word and live His way. We gain more insight into what cannot be seen with the naked eye through the eyes of Christ. **1Corinthians 2:4-5 NIV** – *"My message and preaching were not with wise and persuasive words, but with a demonstration of the Spirit's power, so that your faith might not rest on human wisdom, but on God's power."*

In my younger days I wanted to wear glasses because they were stylish, but I was not wise enough to consider the difference between wanting and needing them. It was fashionable, attractive, and an addition to my appearance, so I thought. I pretended I could not see just to get a new pair of

21

what I assumed looked stylish. Then one day I realized I wasn't pretending, I really needed glasses! Ugh, now the beauty of it all was lost because it was needed, rather than wanted. This required a dependency on something external, which changed my initial view of myself. Trends come and go, but the stability of life requires an understanding of cause and effect as well as the influence of different sources of power.

Decisions or incidents impact our lives differently based on the condition of the heart and the chosen navigator. When God becomes our navigator even what was meant for evil can work out for our good because the purpose is already written in the script. The cause is often greater than the casualty because God's ultimate plan is for his glory and the development of our character. However, these lessons often slip through the cracks of brokenness, anger, and frustration if there is no request for wisdom.

God allows certain things to happen that may be considered traumatic, but in the darkroom of life He develops His wisdom, and character in us. The question at hand is "what is valued the most, godly character or riches? How do I appear to others? How well do I internalize things? Ask the Spirit of God to show you. His light will expose what is hidden from our understanding and He will not just reveal the truth but help you to embrace it in your walk.

PRAY WITH ME

Father, thank you for loving me and your willingness to teach me your ways. Your greatness includes power, and wisdom; therefore, I can trust You when I can't sense your presence. Your journey is not merely a tour of life, but it also includes Your purpose in life. My decision to obey You will prompt me to yield to the directions given in Your word. Detours will only delay my destiny, but You are the pen-writer of time and have already seen and fulfilled my outcome when I follow Your will. Lord, you are not subjected to my days because you created them. I'm sure You can handle my concerns. Lord, help me to release them into Your hands and apply the wisdom that is ready to be released to me.

REFLECTIONS

In your search for truth, what are you able to see more clearly about God and yourself? Write down your thoughts as you read or pray.

_____

_____

_____

_____

_____

_____

_____

_____

_____

_____

_____

_____

_____

DAY 6

Behold, I stand at the door and knock. If anyone hears my voice and opens the door, I will come into him and eat with him, and he with me.

Revelation 3:20 NIV

SOMEONE'S AT THE DOOR!

Christ invites us to open the door to our lives. Can you hear the knocking, but not the voice? Often people knock on our doors, and we pretend not to be home, or we will tip-toe to the peep hole to see who is there, which is a deciding factor whether the door remains closed or open. In this case Christ not only knocks but speaks of his intentions

Doors can be used to enter a personal area or to keep out intruders. They are used to provide safety and security from outside intrusions. We place alarms, motion detectors, and peep holes for protection. Christ the Messiah, knocks and waits at the door of pain, disappointment, struggles, insecurities, brokenness, and other issues that block our ability to hear the truth. **He is waiting. Answer the door!** Unless you open the door to your heart you will not find the truth that brings freedom and real fellowship. **John 14:6 NIV**– Jesus said... *"I am the way, and the truth, and the life. No one comes to the father except through me.*

It is a good day to rebuild our doors with transparency, and with a sense of vulnerability, so we can all be free with purpose. Identify what is in your doorway and give it to Jesus when you open it. I promise He will come in.

MY SECRET PLACE

It can be overwhelming to face challenges, but moments of truth usher the hope of Christ into our hearts. The starting point is to be open and honest, even if it means saying, "I'm not sure and I need God's help." There is more strength in admitting my frailty because it swings open the door for more opportunities.

The open door of transparency allows Christ to come into my messy place, broken heart, and unresolved issues. This world has ongoing issues like false relationships, possessing things, fighting challenges, or covering up brokenness while fighting to reach the top; however, as we humble ourselves and embrace the truth of God's word, Your way and our purpose becomes known. No excuses, blame games, it's just time to lay everything on the table with God who is an expert at resurrecting dead stuff and unlocking doors.

The desire to be open and honest with God is the key that can unlock anyone's door. When a pure heart bows before the Lord it is bendable and willing to follow His lead. It is the pursuit of God's will and righteousness, rather than being flawless or gaining things, that makes room for His presence. God will faithfully reveal his way of doing things. **Jeremiah 29:13 NIV** – *"You will seek me and find me when you seek me with all your heart."* Knowing God without doing life with Christ leaves us stuck behind our own doors; however, the invisible bars of fear cannot hold us hostage once we answer the door and let Him in.

PRAY WITH ME

I declare today that my focus is on God and the positive work He is doing in my life, such as character development, kingdom work, and family. I invite the Spirit of wisdom to take a front seat in my decision-making. As I continually submit to Your will and way. You will empower me to resist the temptation of taking control or choosing other sources.

James 4:7 NIV – *"Submit yourselves, then to God. Resist the devil, and he will flee from you."*

Thank you, Lord, for revealing the truth that shines just enough light on the path where my feet must land. I am humbled by Your greatness in my weakness and Your love in my struggle. This alone compels me to press toward the high calling in Christ. Seeing that you have knocked on my door, I will not only open it, but I am taking all the locks off.

REFLECTIONS

In your search for truth, identify what is in your doorway. Give it to Jesus! Write down your thoughts as you read or pray.

_____

_____

_____

_____

_____

_____

_____

_____

_____

_____

_____

_____

DAY 7

And we all, with unveiled faces, beholding the glory of the Lord, are being transformed into the same image from one degree of glory to another. For this comes from the Lord who is the Spirit.

2 Corinthians 3:18 NIV

UNVEILED TO BE TRANSFORMED

Paul's letter was to people who were no longer in the dark concerning truth which was able to prevail over their issues and circumstances. God's transforming power provides freedom in our areas of struggle. Knowing truth is multi-faceted and will reflect the dominant character of Christ to be seen by others for God's glory.

MY SECRET PLACE

As a bride who lifts her veil before her groom, we open the way to our soul that is anchored by love. **Hebrews 6:19 NIV** *"We have this hope as an anchor for the soul, firm and secure."* Her beauty is not hidden anymore by the scars of her past and the newness of that saving day never fades away. The transforming power of God gracefully covers her scars without removing memories to assure that this day of restoration is kept in her heart and mind.

Can you hear Him calling? Come, my bride. I have waited patiently for your surrender. I have enabled you to soar with Me to higher heights and deeper depths." There is more for you than this world can offer. The yearning to know about the unseen comes from God's Spirit who calls and tugs at your heart and spirit. He is ready to transform your life whenever you are ready to be unveiled. John 14:26 NIV – *"But the Advocate, the Holy Spirit, whom the Father will send in my name, will teach you all things and will remind you of everything I have said to you.*

PRAY WITH ME

Dear Lord, you have rescued me and wiped away my tears. You have caused me to stand in my brokenness and loved me when I did not understand true love. I came to you with many scars and memories I wanted to erase, but You have lifted the veil that kept me in bondage and guilt. I have often felt powerless and stuck in my past. However, You paused the chaos long enough to lift the veil from my eyes, renew my strength, and heal me from the fear of more pain in this world.

You are my portion, my refuge, and my deliverer. Lord, saturate me with Your presence and overwhelm me with the intimacy of knowing more of who You are. Help me to see by faith and understand the outcome of what has already been planned so that I may live in the abundance of Your promises.

REFLECTIONS

<u>In your search for truth, what are you able to see more clearly about God and yourself? Write down your thoughts as you read or pray.</u>

_____

_____

_____

_____

_____

_____

_____

_____

_____

_____

_____

_____

_____

_____

_____

DAY 8

But, as it is written, "What no eye has seen, nor ear heard, nor the heart of man imagined, what God has prepared for those who love him" — these things God revealed to us through the Spirit. For the Spirit searches everything, even the depths of God.

1 Corinthians 2:9-10 NIV

SEEING IS BELIEVING

Neuroscientists have noted that the eyes can only comprehend what the mind can understand and things that are misunderstood are likely to be dismissed or overlooked. The capacity of the natural eye and our hearing has limits. Human eyes cannot capture the speed of light but can only visualize light as it reaches its destination. However, in this scripture, God will reveal to us what our eyes cannot see. One of the ways He communicates to us is by His Spirit to our spirits and He calls us children of light. What we could not see, hear, or imagine before is revealed by His grace and our faith. The Spirit of God searches the heart of man and reveals the truth which is the complete will of God. Now we can see, although in part because He has opened our eyes, and we believe. **Ephesians 5:8 NIV** – *"For you were once darkness, but now you are light in the Lord. Live as children of light"* ...

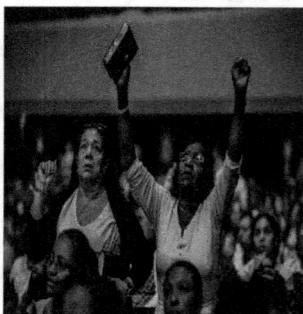

PRAY WITH ME

Father, you are not hiding from me nor are you too busy. You have waited patiently with the knowledge of my tomorrows. My confidence is in You because my eyes have been opened to who You are. This desire for a more profound understanding has stirred my spirit. **Psalms 119:105 NIV** - *"Your word is a lamp for my feet, a light on my path."* Following your path will always provide light so that I may see and hear what the Spirit of the Lord is saying. Your word has repeatedly said, "He who has an ear, let him hear what the Spirit is saying." ...

You are so much bigger than my current circumstances, my yesterday, or my tomorrow. In my time zone, You are limitless, and Your greatness stretches out above the frail world and sees our beginnings and endings at once. Why wouldn't I have confidence in your love for me? I never earned it, nor did I persuade you to love me.

Lord, you are like no other and your plans are beyond my understanding. Therefore, I can face what is bigger than me because your greatness is always before me. Due to my position in Christ, greatness is a part of my life and not something I have done on my own. **Revelations 1:8 NIV** - *"I am the Alpha and the Omega," says the Lord God, "who is, and who was, and who is to come, the Almighty.*

REFLECTIONS

<u>In your search for truth, what are you able to see more clearly about God and yourself? Write down your thoughts as you read or pray.</u>

_____

_____

_____

_____

_____

_____

_____

_____

_____

_____

_____

_____

_____

_____

_____

DAY 9

But let him ask in faith, with no doubting, for the one who doubts is like a wave of the sea that is driven and tossed by the wind. For that person must not suppose that he will receive anything from the Lord; He is a double-minded man, unstable in all his ways.

James 1:6-8 ESV

THE TWO HEADED MONSTER

James speaks of the two-headed monster of being double-minded that every believer must identify with. The way to eliminate this monster requires being true to oneself regarding where our focus is. When our focus is on the secular world, rather than the word of God the process of sanctification is slowed down. Sanctification sets us apart from worldly values and causes us to think and act like Christ. It is a lifetime process! As we slip back and forth between double standards, the winds of life will show that there is a need to grow in truth. God has offered the mind of Christ as a guide for our thoughts. However, the transformation will only take place when we allow the word of God to be the center of our focus. **Philippians 2:5 NIV**- *"In your relationships with one another, have the same mindset as Christ Jesus:"* **The more we meditate on God's word and intentionally apply His word, God's presence and power shows up**. Our discovery of God's greatness and our willingness to make room for Him will usher us into oneness and agreement with His

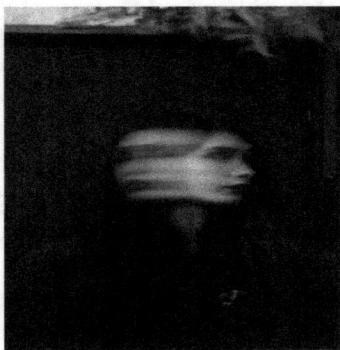

perfect will for creation. The winds come as a measuring device to reveal the level of our faith and to determine if more faith is needed. With increased faith and understanding, God will keep us from being tossed about. Do not worry, He gives power to the weak to stand and a peace that will steady our steps. Other scripture references: **1 Corinthians 2:16, Ephesians 6:13-14**

PRAY WITH ME

Dear Lord, let my reverence for your person and your presence always be with me. Keeping my mind and heart in fellowship with you depends on my awareness of your presence. Today I will think of Your loveliness, goodness, heaven's report of Your glory, and the virtue that flows from Your blood with redeeming power for me. **Philippians 4:8 NIV** – *"Finally, brothers and sisters, whatever is true, whatever is noble, whatever is right, whatever is pure, whatever is lovely, whatever is admirable—if anything is excellent or praiseworthy—think about such things."* **The classroom of life will always assess my faith, and I have often failed, but I will not give up.** Help me to see and hear Your words that I have hidden in my heart when the winds of life blow my way.

Today, I release my thoughts, feelings, and preconceived ideas into your hands. I know Your plans will establish who I am in You and provide freedom to be me. You are my Lord, who has paid a high price that I may live and bring glory to Your name; therefore, I am not my own. Trusting in You enables me to release all into Your hands and will guide me in finding my way to stand in Your presence.

REFLECTIONS

In your search for truth, what are you able to see more clearly about God and yourself? Write down your thoughts as you read or pray.

_____

_____

_____

_____

_____

_____

_____

_____

_____

_____

_____

_____

_____

_____

_____

DAY 10

The words of the mouth are deep waters, but the fountain of wisdom is a rushing stream.

Proverbs 18:4

Restore our fortunes, Lord, like streams in the Negev.

Psalm 126:4

SHALLOW WATERS

Proverbs, the book of profound wisdom describes the substance of our words and their origin. Knowing such wisdom is like standing in streams of gushing waters. Then the psalmist cries out to the Lord to restore our losses, like streams that run through the Negev desert. Who would ask for the impossible, accept by faith and the wisdom of knowing God's unlimited capacity. It is not often that a stream runs through a desert, yet God in his sovereignty can cause the unusual. Treasures are often searched for in deep waters. However, in Proverbs God speaks of wisdom that is greater than the flow of a stream.

A wise investor may recommend for security purposes that a person have at least three streams of income. This is just in case an investment becomes a faulty choice. However, this stream provided by God, flows from rivers of living waters, quenches the thirst of the upright, and makes a way in desert places. The wisdom of God is more than written words in a book or what people would call genius. **Wisdom**

flows like rivers of running water from God causing **movement, direction, and victory even in dry places.** Yes, enough to quench your thirst and strengthen your walk.

In a desert, this stream of water is essential, and when it is from God, there is always an overflow. If you have identified a desert place in your life, look for a stream not made by man. This stream will always move in the direction of its source and will not lead you to something different from His word, nor will it ever run dry.

PRAY WITH ME

Father, I know there are many streams out there to choose from, but I need the one that will cause me to never thirst again. There are many waters to drink from, but some are deceitful. I will turn to the One who created the streams in the desert and who can calm the deep waters. Lord, you are my source, my stream that brings forth living waters.

Your wisdom is waiting for me but has often hidden by of the temptation to walk in my own wisdom. Your ways are different and in a class by themselves. Now that I know this, I will thirst and hunger for Your righteousness. I am ready to receive the abundance of Your wisdom and love until I am satisfied. I am humbled by Your incredible power, and I will stand still at the streams to taste and see that You alone are worthy. **Psalm 34:8 NIV** – *"Taste and see that the Lord is good; blessed is the one who takes refuge in him."*

REFLECTIONS

In your search for truth, what are you able to see more clearly about God and yourself? Write down your thoughts as you read or pray.

_____

_____

_____

_____

_____

_____

_____

_____

_____

_____

_____

_____

_____

_____

_____

_____

_____

DAY 11

But He was wounded for our transgressions, He was bruised for our iniquities; The chastisement for our peace was upon Him, And by His stripes we are healed.

Isaiah 53:5-6

HIDDEN SCARS

Christ gave his life as an acceptable punishment for our sins. As a result of our outward acts of rebellion and disobedience, our Lord suffered with open wounds as his flesh was stripped from his body. Jeusus Christ endured the pain of to take our place and experienced the weight and agony of our sins as he hung on the cross. By his internal bleeding, our hearts is cleansed of the sins residing within. He covered it all, from the inside out, and accepted the punishment that was meant for us to give us peace with God and to be healed.

Wow! Over the years we have acquired scars that tell the story of our past. Like the time I tripped over a ball and damaged a nerve in my front tooth, or the time when an abusive partner knocked my tooth out. There was a time when I was so high, I burned my arm in the oven and did not know it. I thought I had scars for life! Well at least on the outside. Your stories may be different, like when you put all your trust and love into a person and then was abandoned, betrayed, or deeply hurt. Then there's the generational scars of never knowing the love of your biological father and carrying unanswered questions most of your life, like, "Why didn't you love me enough to hang around?" With so many scars it is impossible to hide all of them.

Let's be honest, who wants everyone to see the brokenness and pain we suffer through because of sin? However, Christ left nothing undone with his sacrificial life, and he openly took the scars of our sins on the cross and in the grave. He paid for the pain of those held captive, as well as the cruelty in this world so we can now live in Him. Our scars are hidden in Christ, and His sacrifice gives us inner peace with the Father. Now by faith, every scar has a checkmark of grace and becomes a steppingstone towards wisdom from God, rather than continued torment and pain. **Joel 3:10 NIV** - *Beat your plowshares into swords and your pruning hooks into spears. Let the weakling say, "I am strong!"*

PRAY WITH ME

Thank you, Jesus! You made a way to escape the penalty of sin and did not keep your scars a secret. Your healing and redeeming work on the cross is sufficient for me, and Your love has kept me safe when I had no security around me. Lord. You are my hiding place and you have chosen me as a dwelling place.

Through internalizing what You have done for me, freedom is transforming me from the inside out. It is true that your healing power is real. My scars have become my witness for those who have open wounds or those who have lost hope in their healing process.

We are witnesses of Your grace and mercy that is given freely because of Christ; therefore, I am whole in my weaknesses because You worked it out victoriously on the cross and out from an empty grave. Thank you, Jesus! The scar I carry now is Your cross of redemption. **Ephesians 4:30 AMP** – *"And do not grieve the Holy Spirit of God (but seek to* *please Him), by whom you were sealed and marked (branded as God's own) for the day of redemption (the final deliverance from the consequences of sin)."*

REFLECTIONS

In your search for truth, what are you able to see more clearly about God and yourself? Identify the scars that Christ has healed for your witness. Write down your thoughts as you read or pray.

_____

_____

_____

_____

_____

_____

_____

_____

_____

_____

_____

_____

_____

_____

_____

_____

DAY 12

For all creation is waiting patiently and hopefully for that future day when God will resurrect his children. For on that day thorns and thistles, sin, death, and decay—the things that overcame the world against its will at God's command—will all disappear, and the world around us will share in the glorious freedom from sin which God's children enjoy.

Romans 8:19-21 TLB

WHO'S WAITING ON WHO?

Travelling to work by bus usually requires everyone to be in a long line waiting patiently. We mumbled and complained about the hassle of rushing to get there and facing another delay. There was always an excuse as to why the bus was late and with limited seating the waiting period started over for those who were in the overflow.

Displaying patience while waiting for an answer can be nerve wrecking, yet the word of God mentions that creation is waiting patiently with hope. Is it God who is delaying the matter? Or is His concern to not leave anyone behind a compelling reason for Him to delay a little longer? Every day He waits is another chance for someone else to choose Him as Lord. This entire world is impacted by our sinful and selfish decisions while someone else is in line behind us. As a result of a trail mix of choices, many people suffer and often turn away from God's perfect plan. God in His infinite power and wisdom knows when He will no longer need to wait.

There will be an end to current suffering, and horrible delays, but only He knows the fullness of time. In the meantime, God displays short trailers in this world that give notice that the waiting period is winding up.

Do not be late or slothful! Be willing to share with others the hope that you have found and the glorious freedom from sin. Stay in His will while serving and trust His will to be done! God is waiting, creation is waiting, but time waits for no one, and the means of transportation will not be late.

PRAY WITH ME

Father, thank you for sounding the alarm in my life and freeing me from peer pressure, insecurities, and all the struggles that keep me from getting closer to you. While I wait, I will serve, and I refuse to be part of the delay any longer. You made a way for me to escape the snares of life; and today, I choose to walk in the liberty of Christ.

My decision is final, and I will not change it. You have the power to keep me and deliver me from all evil. My clock is ticking, and I hear the alarm. I will rise and give you glory with my life and someone else will hear and be awakened. The body of Christ will rise together and press towards the prize by Your grace that we may please You. **Philippians 3:14 NIV** – *"I press on toward the goal to win the prize for which God has called me heavenward in Christ Jesus."* There will be another time of peace on earth and creation will no longer groan because we will behold Your glory.

REFLECTIONS

In your search for truth, what are you able to see more clearly about God and yourself? What has delayed you in your walk in Christ? Write down your thoughts as you read or pray.

_____

_____

_____

_____

_____

_____

_____

_____

_____

_____

_____

_____

_____

_____

_____

_____

_____

_____

_____

DAY 13

But if serving the Lord seems undesirable to you, then choose for yourselves this day whom you will serve, whether the gods your ancestors served beyond the Euphrates, or the gods of the Amorites, in whose land you are living. But as for me and my household, we will serve the Lord."

Joshua 24:15 NIV

PRO-CHOICE?

Joshua declared that nothing and no one could change his commitment to God. He knew he would not be able to convince everyone to commit their lives to God, but he took the responsibility to lead his family to do the same. Joshua understood the negative impact of culture, and the act of idolatry that persuaded past generations to worship other gods. His commitment to God changed Joshua's heart towards God; therefore, he allowed God's greatness, holiness, and His rule to guide him. His choice was without question

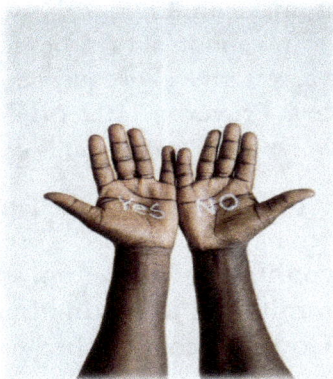

Choices are all around us. We live in a world that screams personal rights, preferences, and pro-choice. America, the land of freedom! The enforcement of laws was not meant for those who keep the law, but for the lawless. God gave the ten commandments to set boundaries between righteousness and evil based on His judgement and for our protection.

When boundaries are moved, choices multiply and often become corrupt and lawless. God did not take away our right to choose. The choice is still there, but the problem remains when the wrong decision leads to consequences. To live by God's standards and truths from the written word will always produce far better results than a person's feelings, or opinions. Who is wiser? Remember a choice is always at hand!

The choice of your source for answers will be based on your values. God our creator is wiser, stronger, and has more integrity than man's capability. The truth of the matter is it is easier to reach across to someone close for direction rather than make an effort to be stretched where the prize is. True victory cannot always be seen unless it is revealed by the truth, yet the consequences of wrong choices trail behind deceit. **Proverbs 14:12 NIV-** *"There is a way that appears to be right, but in the end, it leads to death."*

Joshua chose to be an example for those who were watching his life as a servant to the Highest. **Being accountable does not require perfection, but a commitment to getting back up.** When you fall your trust in God must continue because his unchanging love will guide, correct, and empower you to overcome. The choice is yours. Just know that God is an expert at loving in difficult places.

PRAY WITH ME

Father, thank you for loving me through my right and wrong choices. Although the consequences were difficult, Your love and grace sustained me. Your instructions are clear on how to live, with the promise to complete this good work in my life that You started. **Philippians 1:6 NIV**- *"being confident of this, that he who began a good work in you will carry it on to completion until the day of Christ Jesus."*

Please remove any false love that portrays false hope from my life. Anything that distracts or takes up my time from being who you said I am will no longer have a preference. You are my first love, and the only one who has standards not set by man.

Give me a clean heart and grace me with Your favor in this fresh start. **Psalms 51:10 NIV** – *"Create in me a pure heart, O God, and renew a steadfast spirit within me."* I have broken so many promises, but I know that You will keep all of yours; therefore, when I fall, I will get back up again. You said in Your word, *"For though the righteous fall seven times, they rise again,"* - **Proverbs 24:16 NIV** Today, I commit my life to You, and You have declared me righteous. This request is not just for me, but for all those watching, and I pray they realize we can all make it. Thank you for choosing me, now my choice is to trust You.

REFLECTIONS

In your search for truth, what are you able to see more clearly about God and yourself? Write down your thoughts as you read or pray.

_____

_____

_____

_____

_____

_____

_____

_____

_____

_____

_____

_____

_____

_____

DAY 14

Then the devil took him to the holy city and had him stand on the highest point of the temple. "If you are the Son of God," he said, "throw yourself down. For it is written: "He will command his angels concerning you, and they will lift you up in their hands, so that you will not strike your foot against a stone." Jesus answered him, "It is also written: 'Do not put the Lord your God to the test."

Matthew 4:5-7 NIV

TESTING IN PROGRESS

When a test is scheduled, a person must take time to prepare; however, we often habitually wait until the last minute to cram and review the subject matter. This terrible habit can put the smartest person in a bind, especially since the teacher is silent during the test, yet the same behavior may continue.

Hopefully, we can learn the significance of prioritizing and preparing while observing how Jesus prepared for a test that many people needed Him to pass.

The word of God indicates that Jesus fasted for 40 days and then was led into the wilderness where the Spirit of God tested him. He was tested in three areas that every believer must currently face, which include the following: **The lust of the flesh** – A self-centered desire to please oneself at any cost for self-satisfaction. **The lust of the eyes** - a desire for what looks attractive and appealing at any cost. **The pride of life -**

Anything or anyone who is highly regarded (including self) or valued more than the standards of God.

Jesus was physically weak during this temptation test because he had abstained from eating; however, the discipline of His human nature provided strength to His Spirit. He understood the struggle and was able to respond in His Spirit which will always reflect the will of His Father. **1 Timothy 1:7 NIV** – *"For the Spirit God gave us does not make us timid, but gives us power, love and self-discipline."*

Encountering fear, and uncertainties in life as well as not knowing who we are in Christ can cause a person to be vulnerable to the weaknesses of our sinful nature. Jesus' temptation tests were in the same areas we face today and prepping for the test should be part of our lifestyle. Studying and knowing the written word of God and hiding it in our hearts as we examine ourselves will assure us that Christ is ruling. When we apply truth to our decisions it is a very effective way of preparation

Know this: just as we depended on Christ to pass the test, someone is depending on you to pass. Be proactive, prepare! God will do the rest. Besides it's an open book test, but you may not want to wait or have time to get the book. Hide it in your heart. You need to be sure you have a graceful helper. Holy Spirit it's Your turn!

PRAY WITH ME

Thank you, Lord, for clearing the path and showing me how to overcome the temptations of the world. Despite the fact that my busyness has cluttered and delayed my progress with useless things, I am grateful it did not invalidate the work You called me to do for the kingdom. In the classroom of temptation, I am ready to let go, remove, and even leave behind the things of old that try to ensnare me.

My decision to follow Christ sets me on the path to be led by His response to every temptation, "It is written." Help me to prepare by studying the word of God so that truth and love reside in my heart. You have provided everything for the test and although some are more difficult than others, you have pre-graded them all with a "V" for victory and a curve in the grade because of "grace." **2 Corinthians 12:9NIV** – *"But he said to me, "My grace is sufficient for you, for my power is made perfect in weakness."* Thank you for your strength in my weakness. It is my understanding that if I am willing to follow you to the cross, it will lead me to victory.

REFLECTIONS

In your search for truth, what are you able to see more clearly about God and yourself? Write down your thoughts as you read or pray.

_____

_____

_____

_____

_____

_____

_____

_____

_____

_____

_____

DAY 15

Never take your own revenge, beloved, but leave room for the wrath of God, for it is written: "Vengeance is mine, I will repay." Says the Lord.

Romans 12:19 NASB

THE MISDIRECTED PUNCH!

Growing up as an only child my mom always told me not to fear anyone and to fight to protect myself. Unfortunately, the day that a bully in my third-grade class decided to take a swing at me, I swung as hard as I could, but the teacher got in the way. Boy was I in trouble! No one asked who started the fight or my intentions because the focus was on my misguided punch and the damage I caused. Although the bully never bothered me again, I had slayed the wrong giant.

The word of God instructs us to not take matters into our own hands and to have confidence God can manage the issues in our lives. However, in the heat of the moment we are tempted to defend ourselves and miss the realization that there's more at stake than can be seen. Other bystanders may get hurt in the process or someone may be learning how to handle life from your actions without your knowledge. An old African proverb says, "When elephants fight it's the grass that always suffers." Someone is always watching but most importantly **God is watching and waiting for your love and trust in Him to be greater than your anger.** **Ephesians 4:26-27 NIV** – *"In your anger do not sin. Do not let*

the sun go down while you are still angry and do not give the devil a foothold."

PRAY WITH ME

Father, I have not always understood your ability to hold back your anger, but I have certainly benefited from it. Thank you for your mercy, Lord, for holding back deserving consequences and demonstrating the depth of your love. I know I have chosen actions at times that angered You. Your love and purpose keep me alive, even though many others did not recover from the same wrong decisions.

I am asking that You grace me with the same mindset as Christ for the sake of my audience who may emulate my actions. The discipline of our emotions is significantly needed because our sons and daughters are watching, but I know this can only be accomplished by You. They are our legacy, and part of Your kingdom. Less I forget the possibility of others who You have placed in my path and their need to see my witness of Your greatness.

If I show my strength without You, I have prematurely jumped up before the bell rings and left my greatness behind. Your strength is unfailing when I follow Your lead and put my trust in You. Help me to aim for the prize of the high calling in Christ, so that my punch will never be misguided. Thank you, Lord, for the victory! Yeah, I know it is such a different kind of fight. **Philippians 3:14 NIV** – *"I press on toward the goal to win the prize for which God has called me heavenward in Christ Jesus."*

REFLECTIONS

In your search for truth, what are you able to see more clearly about God and yourself? Write down your thoughts as you read or pray.

_____

_____

_____

_____

_____

_____

_____

_____

_____

_____

_____

_____

_____

_____

_____

DAY 16

And he said to him, "You shall love the Lord your God with all your heart and with all your soul and with all your mind.

Matthew 22:37 NIV

LOVE BUGS

Jesus pointed out the first greatest commandment to one of the Pharisees was to identify other existing loves and admonish the love of God as a priority. The heart, soul, and mind in its entirety must have the same values concerning God's love. Other love relationships can influence or cause deception in a person's life if trust is in the wrong place. That is why we *confess with our mouth and believe with our heart...* - **Romans 10:9**, *and hope is an anchor for the soul, firm and secure...* - **Hebrews 6:19**, *"and may the God who gives perseverance and encouragement grant you to be of the same mind with one another, according to Christ Jesus,"* - **Romans 15:5**. These passages clearly show the significant role the mind, soul and heart play in our relationship with God.

Once a decision is made to engage in a relationship the desire to be loved without force is always there. In a relationship, love should be the motivator and factor in making decisions, responding, and acting. Now we know this doesn't always happen, yet our love for God and for one another will often cause a sliding scale if other lovers exist. No worries, this is not weird thinking, but the yearning taste of worldly love will conflict with the love of Christ. There is no room for both! Either one will be removed or devalued. They take up space and time that was only meant for your

Father. **Matthew 6:24 NIV** - *No one can serve two masters. Either you will hate the one and love the other, or you will be devoted to the one and despise the other. You cannot serve both God and money."*

We develop various love bugs based on our upbringing, painful experiences, sinful nature, or the level of love we have for ourselves and God. These old bugs usually surface when choices are at hand. Calling them love bugs is not an indication that they are beneficial, but lovable enough to draw us into sin. Shining God's light on these bugs will expose the love of money, fame, and fortune, selfishness, idolatry, and being in control. The infestation of these bugs is distracting to the life of a Christian and an intrusion into any relationship.

There will be a time when promises and the wonderful commitments made at the altar to man or to God require action. Love bugs, without making light of the matter, are outside priorities that destroy relationships or limit relationships with God. These bugging desires dwell within the heart or mind, taking up space that should not be vacant. While the soul is anchored in Christ, the commitment of the heart, and renewing of the mind is based on the level of surrender. Love is a decision, not just a pleasant feeling. God has already decided, but He waits for us.

PRAY WITH ME

Thank you, Lord, for always being near even when the struggle is real to end these old bug affairs. You are faithful, and Your strength is beyond measure. The word of God tells me to have confidence in the work that You began in me and will finish. Although change hurts I will adapt to Your ways because You know my past before I begin. Please exterminate these old bugs of anger, rejection, idolatry, and any open doors from my past.

Lord, help me to break the cycle. Today I will emerge from the revolving door! I choose to give You the keys to my heart, mind, and soul because You have graciously loved me. Lord, I invite you into every vacant space in my life and will honor your presence, and authority to lead me on the path of righteousness.

You thought of me when I was too busy and mired in old stuff that crowded my mind and prevented me from a life of freedom. Thanks to Your greatness, I can now truly dedicate my life to You and leave the old things behind. **Romans 6:6 NIV-** *"For we know that our old self was crucified with him so that the body ruled by sin might be done away with, that we should no longer be slaves to sin."*

REFLECTIONS

In your search for truth, what are you able to see more clearly about God and yourself? Write down your thoughts as you read or pray.

_____

_____

_____

_____

_____

_____

_____

_____

_____

_____

DAY 17

…. the appearing of our Lord Jesus Christ, which he will display at the proper time – he who is the blessed and only Sovereign, the King of kings and Lord of lords,

1 Timothy 6:14b-15 ESV

EXPECTING SOMEONE?

God has an appointed time for everything and knows the events of every tomorrow. Our view of what is needed in life is based on experience, preference, and culture while God's view has a much better scope on things. He sees the intentions of the heart and has a plan to accomplish His will.

It is God's appointed time for everything, and He knows what will happen tomorrow. Our view of what is needed in life is based on experience, preference, and culture while God's view has a much better scope on things. He sees the intentions of the heart and has a plan to accomplish His will.

Since the timing of the return of Christ is unknown to man, it is often not considered by people. Instead, it is placed on the backburner of our minds while events continue to happen like flags of warning. If we really knew when that day was approaching, many of us would work hard preparing for that day as if it were a hot date. Putting on our Sunday finest, cleaning up and catching up on all our unfinished business, as if God didn't see our current state.

In medieval times, kings ruled with dominion in a specific land, and lords helped to govern the people, but in this scripture, Christ is declared as ruler overall. Therefore, the timing of his return is not based on a power struggle for territory, but His love and patience for us.

Not ready yet? Getting ready? Or it's on my to do list. How about, let's do it? The choice is yours, but when His time comes around, tomorrow ends and it will be too late. **Revelations1:3** *"Blessed is the one who reads aloud the words of this prophecy and blessed are those who hear it and take to heart what is written in it, because the time is near."*

PRAY WITH ME

Father, forgive me for often falling into the simple trap of thinking I have time. Some people have missed the chance to change because their last chapter popped up without warning. Help me to remember that the gift of life allows me to live in the present. As a loving Father, you have waited for many of us to stop procrastinating or making excuses for not committing our lives to You.

I acknowledge Your faithfulness, diligence, and patience while darkness was not just around me, but in me. Your greatness made my soul an eternal priority, and I declare that I will give You the same place in my heart. You are more than a friend, or the man upstairs. You are my maker, keeper, and lover of my soul. **Psalms 42:1 NIV** – *"As the deer pants for streams of water, so my soul pants for you, my God."* I will prepare for Your return with more than just a quick clean-up. Today I embrace who You are, and Your faithfulness. Yes, let this be a time of awakening to know there is much to do and accomplish.

REFLECTIONS

In your search for truth, what are you able to see more clearly about God and yourself? Being true to yourself is the greatest start to victory. Write down your thoughts as you read or pray.

_____

_____

_____

_____

_____

_____

_____

_____

_____

_____

_____

_____

_____

_____

_____

DAY 18

For God speaks in one way, and in two, though man does not perceive it. In a dream, in a vision of the night, when deep sleep falls on men, while they slumber on their beds.

Job 33:14-15 ESV

CAN YOU SEE WHAT I'M SAYING?

Growing up, I was taught never to give back-talk when being disciplined, and submissively I did not speak. Oh, but my thoughts were easy to read on my facial expressions or body gestures. Being Transparent was not one of my issues! You know, those eyes would stretch and roll, or arms would fold, then gravity would slam stuff down in the room. Of course, this led to more intimate conversations of understanding which clearly made the initial message understood.

Job recognized God has diverse ways of speaking and the importance of continuing his search for answers since he knew the likelihood of him missing the message. The issue with hearing God is not about the ways He has chosen to speak, but the frequency and condition of our hearts when tuning in to hear Him. God has chosen a number of ways to reach our hearts no matter what is going on!

God speaks through scriptures, spiritually mature people, circumstances, dreams, and visions, and often in a quiet voice. In all these ways of reaching our hearts the noise on

the inside can be the greatest distraction. The importance of knowing and practicing being still will greatly contribute to hearing God and knowing it is Him. **Psalm 37:7 NIV** – *"Be still before the Lord and wait patiently for him;"* ...

. When we listen and embrace God's word it brings forth light to truth that gives us understanding and allows us to see what is being said. **Psalm 119:105 NIV** – *"Your word is a lamp for my feet, a light on my path."*

The word of God says His ways are different from our logical thoughts or ways. **Isaiah 55:8 NIV** - *"For my thoughts are not your thoughts, neither are your ways my ways,"* declares the *Lord."* However, since He knew us before our conception, and the development of our hearing is connected to the reconciling power of God that brings communication to the forefront of our willingness to move and grow. Since His presence eliminates noise makers, the closer we get, the less likely there will be distractions.

PRAY WITH ME

Thank you, Father, for giving me access to hear you, and the power to follow Your instructions. Your ways are different from anything in this world. However, as I press in to get closer to You, my understanding becomes clearer, and I realize there is always more. Make Your ways plain to me so that I may see and hear the truth as You speak. I invite Your Spirit into my thoughts so that I may experience the presence of Your power through Your word. My purpose here is not to boast of knowledge, but to align my life with Your will and to help someone else. I am ready to let Your word accomplish what it was sent to do. **Isaiah 55:11 NIV** – *"...so is my word that goes out from my mouth: It will not return to me empty but will accomplish what I desire and achieve the purpose for which I sent it."*

Understanding Your ways can be challenging, but those who love You in return will experience the work You promised to complete for Your purpose and glory. When

You speak, creation happens, and it responds to Your intentional plans. Keep me so close that the stillness of my soul will invite You to dwell in the chambers of my heart. The sound of Your voice reveals Your character and love, which causes movement and change. Speak Lord, your servant is listening!

My own reasoning will not reach the required level to overcome the challenges in life. Your Spirit examines the debts of Your heart and will bring understanding and power to me to complete Your will. In my journey to discover, ask to understand, and knock to gain access to your chambers, I hope to understand Your ways. Thank you for the invitation and putting up with my many rainchecks. Your patience has been gracious to me.

REFLECTIONS

In your search for truth, what have you discovered about God and yourself? Write down your thoughts as you read or pray

_____

_____

_____

_____

_____

_____

_____

_____

DAY 19

"What do you think? There was a man who had two sons. He went to the first and said, "Son, go and work today in the vineyard." "I will not," he answered, but later he changed his mind and went. "Then the father went to the other son and said the same thing. He answered, "I will, sir," but he did not go. "Which of the two did what his father wanted?"

Matthew 21:28-31a NIV

I CHANGED MY MIND

Jesus told stories to his followers to bring understanding to his messages. This parable points to the response given by the farmer's sons and the conflict pertaining to their actions. At the end of the story Christ told his listeners the tax collectors and the prostitutes would get into the kingdom of God before them. Jesus declared this would happen although the fact that their initial response was a "no," because their final actions became a "yes." **Therefore, the struggle to do what is right or experiencing a rough start will not keep you out of heaven as much as your ending response that is portrayed by your actions. Jeremiah 17:9-10 NIV –** *"The heart is deceitful above all things and beyond cure. Who can understand it? "I the Lord search the heart and examine the mind, to reward each person according to their conduct, according to what their deeds deserve."*

It is certainly an issue if words are spoken based on what we think people want to hear and our efforts were only to please others for that moment. God examines our hearts with truth and can identify deception better than we can. Commitments are made with our mouths while our hearts are still processing the necessities. In haste, the answer may sound appropriate, but without action it is of no value. We lose purpose if we place a greater value on the sound of our response than on obedience to God.

The way of repentance is known when a person's mind has changed about who Christ is in their life, and a change of behavior follows. If He is Lord, then you will allow Him to rule, and you will follow.

Of course, God prefers yes in both cases. It is through grace that we can allow our minds and behavior to move in the same direction as Christ. As the body of Christ, we can also help each other if we work together. Find someone to help. It will strengthen your walk.

Isaiah 43:10 NIV – *"You are my witnesses," declares the Lord, and my servant whom I have chosen, so that you may know and believe me and understand that I am he. Before me no god was formed, nor will there be one after me."*

PRAY WITH ME

Heavenly Father, there is an inside struggle when part of me says yes, and another part says no. The struggle is real because I want to please you with my entire life, but I need Your help. In this struggle, I realize I am alive in Christ and that You have awakened my conscience, as I am no longer blind and lost. Only You know the intentions of my heart. Lord, you promised to be with me and never leave me. This is my confidence! I am confident in Your love, power, and wisdom, but it is me who I often question.

I surrender everything to Your hands including thoughts that don't always line up with Your truth. You are strong even in my weakness, and Your greatness can withstand the cares of this world. I am an overcomer by the blood of Jesus and my testimony of faith in You will not change. You are my hiding place, a mighty fortress. Thank you for being exactly what I needed. Thank you for the opportunity to change my mind.

REFLECTIONS

In your search for truth, what have you discovered about God and yourself? Write down your thoughts as you read and pray

_____

_____

_____

_____

_____

_____

_____

_____

_____

_____

_____

_____

DAY 20

Do not store up for yourselves treasures on earth, where moth and rust destroy, and where thieves break in and steal, but lay up for yourselves treasures in heaven, where neither moth nor rust destroys and where thieves do not break in and steal.

Matthew 6:19-20 ESV

TRINKETS OR TREASURES

Beautiful pieces of jewelry that appeared to be valuable, but only cost a small fortune, sat in the jewelry box, glittering brightly to catch the attention of many. Then one day while reaching in the box an invasion of green mold appeared, and the beauty was lost. These once admired pieces of jewelry were tossed into the box of forgotten old favorites. Occasionally an urge to wear these trinkets would occur, but the dull appearance ruined the gesture. What was once valuable was now tossed into the pile of worthlessness. **What would happen if we could see the mold and dullness of our old lives when we tried to wear them again?**

Following Christ can certainly change a person's perspective on values. And what was once cherished loses its value. Worldly goals usually point to accumulating things and holding onto them. This means your net worth is admired, but when your valuables disappear, your stock takes a dive, even in the eyes of many people.

Our eyes can trick us into believing something is more valuable than its true worth. The word of God assures us that a solid foundation can be found and built on Christ in order that it might last. "Only one life, 'twill soon be past; only what's done for Christ will last." (Missionary C.T. Studd)

Trinkets are easy to come by but hold a small value; however, the treasures of heaven remain certified by the maker. The treasures of godliness, patience, love, holiness, kindness, truth, and much more are given freely, but cost a high price. These treasures will never corrode or fade away because God is the source. Let's clean out the trinket box in our hearts and minds. Better yet, let's just get rid of that storage space. **Colossians 3:1 NIV** – *"Since, then, you have been raised with Christ, set your hearts on things above, where Christ is, seated at the right hand of God."*

PRAY WITH ME

Father thank you for freely providing the authentic treasures of heaven that have more value than what the world offers. Your words tell us to set our affections on things above and not on earthly things. Tangible things will not always be there or valued but the treasures You have given are eternal. **2Corinthians 4:18 NIV** – *"So we fix our eyes not on what is seen, but on what is unseen, since what is seen is temporary, but what is unseen is eternal."*

Thank you for displaying your treasures through Jesus Christ. Only through Him can I obtain them. Help me identify the trinkets I collected on my journey that need to be thrown away. When I open my box of what I deem valuable, I will place it in Your hands, letting Your light shine on any true treasures. Everything You give I will hold in high esteem and allow Your truth to prevail in my heart and mind. With confidence in You they will not fade away. While I am here on earth, I intend to soar toward heaven's treasures.

REFLECTIONS

In your search for truth, what have you discovered about God and yourself? Write down your thoughts as you read or pray.

_____

_____

_____

_____

_____

_____

_____

_____

_____

_____

_____

_____

_____

_____

_____

DAY 21

For the gate is narrow and the way is hard that leads to life, and those who find it are few. John 14:6 — Jesus said to him, "I am the way, and the truth, and the life. No one comes to the father except through me."

Matthew 7:14 ESV

TAKE THE LEAD

As this scripture points out, God wants us to follow His path in an unusual and challenging way that differs from normal ways of living. This road is unpopular and does not offer multiple choice. However, following the guidelines will help us stay on course

Being married provides an interesting experience when riding in the car with your spouse. The husband grips the steering wheel and leads the way, and the wife often sits there on pins and needles wanting to give directions. When she fails to let him lead, the battle begins.

The next ride she decides to entertain herself or enjoy the scenery, and then she discovers they are not traveling the right way. Now she's just busting at the seams to say something when it's a perfect time to practice long suffering or enjoy a peaceful time of prayer.

The funny part about this ride is the husband has no problem listening to the lady on the GPS, perhaps because she's not his wife. **Genesis 3:16b AMP**- *"Yet your desire and longing will be for your husband, and he will rule [with authority] over you and be responsible for you."* Interestingly, once his wife starts giving directions the husband's response is "even if it is a different way, let me do it!"

Is it possible that God gives the same response to our complaints about the route He chooses? Just because it's different from your choice doesn't make it wrong. Then let's buckle up, enjoy the ride, and trust the driver. God certainly knows the way and has a planned destination.

Relationships always clash when two people try to lead. Accidents happen when we ask God to direct us, but grab hold of the steering wheel later because it's an unfamiliar route. His ways are different from ours, and the decision to follow must be made by a mind that is willing to be led.

The miraculous thing is that God does not rush to take the wheel. He waits for an invitation. To reach the destination safely, the driver will not switch seats while moving. Let God take the lead and you don't have to become preoccupied with the scenery to keep your composure. Keep your eyes on Him, not the road. He will give you an understanding of why He took you on this specific route. He always has a plan and a purpose.

PRAY WITH ME

Oh, how wonderful to find rest in our Lord while you take hold of the course of my life. I admit there are times I'm tempted to reach over and be in control. Remind me that You have already been to my next destination, next moment, tomorrow, and days to come. You are not confined to my present time, and Your plans are righteous and not evil; therefore, I will trust You to lead me. **Jeremiah 29:11 NIV –** *"For I know the plans and thoughts that I have for you,' says the Lord, 'plans for peace and well-being and not for disaster, to give you a future and a hope."* My eyes and heart are fixed on You, rather than the changing scenery of life. You hold my heartfelt fears in Your hands, where I find strength. Father, wherever You lead me, it will be right for my faith, which requires trust. Take the lead, while I rest in the comfort of who You are.

REFLECTIONS

In your search for truth, what have you discovered about God and yourself? Write down your thoughts as you read or pray.

_____

_____

_____

_____

_____

_____

_____

_____

_____

_____

_____

_____

DAY 22

If you, Lord, kept a record of sins, Lord, who could stand? But with you there is forgiveness, so that we can, with reverence, serve you. I wait for the Lord, my whole being waits, and in his word, I put my hope.

Psalm 130:3-5 NIV

HEAVEN'S RECORDKEEPING

The psalmist cries out to the Lord and recognizes the dilemma we would be in if God did not forgive man. Unforgiveness will result in a lack of hope. If He kept a record of our wrongdoings no one would be able to approach such a holy God or have fellowship with Him. God provided a way to be forgiven through Christ with His purpose in mind and initiated it as part of His plan. **Fellowship with a holy God allows His presence to affect all of who we are and hope to be.** The Lord gave us life so that we might represent Him in all His holiness and love and not just in one way. The psalmist realized the whole structure of this relationship is about God and his plan for man to have fellowship with Him and to serve Him with honor.

Since man has committed so many sins that need forgiveness, if God was unforgiving there would be no end to our separation from our Father, a holy God. God and man could not have the kind of relationship He desired. To resolve this matter, God has provided a way to restore our fellowship with Him and has given specific instructions like confession, repentance, and forgiving others through Christ.

This plan of restoration includes forgiving ourselves of our misconceived ideas that often led us to wrong paths. God does not instruct us without participating in the process and exemplifies the way to freedom through His son Jesus Christ. Love destroys records of wrongdoings! And in the pain of forgiveness, it is love from the Father that brings forth power to destroy the records of wrongs. **1Corinthians 13:4-5 NIV** – *"Love is patient, love is kind. It does not envy, it does not boast, it is not proud. It does not dishonor others, it is not self-seeking, it is not easily angered, it keeps no record of wrongs."*

True fellowship with the Father will always include forgiveness and in return our heartfelt act of forgiveness allows a person to receive the same love God extended to us. The grudge is forgotten! Holding on is not worth it or an option. Now by His grace, my fellowship with the Father will heal and deliver us from the pain of sin and make us whole to serve effectively. For God's glory, we will destroy the records and make more room for Your dwelling power and wisdom!

PRAY WITH ME

God, there have been times when I thought I had forgiven someone but the moment the offender came near me my posture, attitude, and continence changed. The air appeared thick and uncomfortable. **I realized the idea of forgiveness had come and gone because my heart was still torn; therefore, the pain had trapped my decision to forgive.**

Today, I'm asking You to heal and remove the pain of disappointment, betrayal, and often anger. **The feelings I have are not my whole self and will be subject to Your will as to what is right.** You are my healer and my deliverer. I want to forgive others because You told me to, and You forgave me. I need a clear path to reach You and holding these grudges blocks my fellowship with You. **Psalm 66:18 NIV** – *"If I regard wickedness in my heart, The Lord will not hear,"*

You are a consuming fire; therefore, I invite You to burn up the records in my mind and deliver me from all evil thoughts. Father, only you can heal my heart then You will hear my heart and make ways that I may hear You.

My fellowship with you is worth forgiving others and it will launch me into true purpose. **Ephesians 4:32 NIV** – *"Be kind and compassionate to one another, forgiving each other, just as in Christ God forgave you."* Let my love for You be greater than any emotion or pain that I have endured.

The temptations of this world will not stop me from obeying or having fellowship with You in Jesus' name. Nothing is that serious! You called me to be an overcomer and by Your grace I am, and I'll leave the recordkeeping to You. **Mark 11:25 NIV** – *"And when you stand praying, if you hold anything against anyone, forgive them, so that your Father in heaven may forgive you your sins."*

REFLECTIONS

In your search for truth, what have you discovered about God and yourself? Write down your thoughts as you read or pray.

_____

_____

_____

_____

_____

_____

_____

_____

_____

_____

_____

_____

_____

_____

_____

_____

_____

DAY 23

The Spirit clearly says that in later times some will abandon the faith and follow deceiving spirits and things taught by demons. Such teachings come through hypocritical liars, whose consciences have been seared as with a hot iron.

1 Timothy 4:1-2 NIV

TWISTED TRUTH

The word of God states that, Jesus rebuked the Pharissees and pointed out that the devil is a deceiver, and the father of lies. **John 8:44 NIV** – *"You belong to your father, the devil and you want to carry out your father's desires. He was a murderer from the beginning, not holding to the truth, for there is no truth in him. When he lies, he speaks his native language, for he is a liar and the father of lies."* The devil will strategically use deceptive ways to lure us into traps based on situations and the condition of our hearts. Our lack of understanding these tactics can often be our downfall because they are not always obvious. Moreover, misdirected trust or desires may lead us to believe a lie.

In my younger days, being alone, broken, and feeling like no one cared, or understood me, and the fact that I was desperate to be loved, led me in many wrong directions. Since I grew up in church, strategically the enemy used someone I knew from church who led me further away from God's plan for me. Without all the details, I considered the person trustworthy because of our past environment, rather than

their character. Not only did I not know, but it was deception at its finest, yet I was still responsible for who I chose to put my trust in.

Sometimes, we think we've hit rock bottom when, it was only a pit stop. I needed the Lord in my life, but the enemy sent a counterfeit, yet God's plans will always provide a redemptive alternative.

The devil's goal is always to kill, steal, and destroy, but his strategies are often handpicked based on our weaknesses, pains, and vulnerable hearts that lack truth. **John 10:10 NIV** – *"The thief comes only to steal and kill and destroy; I came so that they would have life and have it abundantly."*

There is only one truth, and the absence of truth iis an inviting platform for a lie that can leads to destruction. The opportunity to escape by grace is an open door for wisdom, rather than regret. It wasn't my first mistake, nor was it the last, but grace and mercy turned them into steppingstones to reach higher and become stronger in the Lord. Yes, wisdom will help us not to repeat that class again. Get up! Who's counting if you get up again? **Proverbs 24:16 NIV** – *"For a righteous person falls seven times and rises again, But the wicked stumble in time of disaster."*

PRAY WITH ME

Father, thank you for not letting my mistakes devour my purpose. Your amazing love has rescued me. Many people may not tell the story, but my gratefulness will not permit my silence. There is no error or sin that the blood of Jesus is not capable of covering. **Ephesians 2:13 NIV** – *"But now in Christ Jesus you who previously were far away have been brought near by the blood of Christ. You know my going out and coming in."*

The lack of wisdom and not being united with You came close to my destruction, but You made a way of escape through Christ. Now I ask that You endow me with Your wisdom as I reverently stand in agreement with Your way of life for me. Lord, I will honor and worship you with my obedience in this walk and although I may stumble again, you are faithful. **Isaiah 1:19 NIV** – *"If you are willing and obedient, you will eat the best of the land;"* ... I know You will help me to get back up again because my decision is to walk in kingdom purpose, rather than my personal wants.

Your glory in my life will speak louder than my voice and defend me from my accusers. Thank You for the love that will eliminate the fear of making another mistake. **2Timothy 1:7 NLT** – *"For God has not given us a spirit of fear and timidity, but of power, love, and self-discipline"* My confidence is in who You are, and it is enough to motivate me to live for Your purpose. Thank you for strength and the fresh breeze that blows in the newness of life. **Romans 6:4 NASB** – *"Therefore we have been buried with Him through baptism into death, so that, just as Christ was raised from the dead through the glory of the Father, so we too may walk in newness of life."*

REFLECTIONS

In your search for truth, what have you discovered about God and yourself? Write down your thoughts as you read or pray.

_____

_____

_____

_____

_____

_____

_____

_____

_____

_____

_____

_____

_____

_____

_____

_____

_____

_____

DAY 24

Then he returned to his disciples and found them sleeping. "Simon, "he said to Peter, "are you asleep? Couldn't you keep watch for one hour? Watch and pray so that you will not fall into temptation. The spirit is willing, but the flesh is weak."

Mark 14:37-38 NIV

CAN HE TRUST ME WITH TROUBLE?

During Christ's walk among us the above scripture describes one of the most painful moments he had to endure. Unjustly, he was about to face death in a horrific way. To make matters worse, His disciples slept through His time of agony but claimed they loved Him and would be loyal. Christ did not let the shortcomings of His disciples lose sight of His purpose. Instead, He instructed them to pray for each other, rather than for himself. To see them slumbering in weakness during the urgent need for prayer spoke volumes of man's weakness and why Christ had to overcome sin, death, and the grave. **Yes, these later to be mighty men of God slept through the birthing of a crisis, and some denied knowing Christ in the time of persecution.** Thank God for grace!

The frailty of man is clear to see, "frantic in a storm, and sleep before the crucifixion." Without being so critical of the disciples, let's admit many of us have slept through someone's crisis. However, we frantically call on the name of the Lord when it hits home.

During my prayer life, the question was often posed "Can I trust you with the trouble?" My immediate response was "uh oh, what trouble?" but the trouble wasn't what I thought but it was concerning someone else, rather than myself. Will you value another persons' needs as much as yours to stay up or to get up early and pray? When you discover their struggles, weaknesses, and pain, will you stay and pray without talking about them later? **It is easy to see the weaknesses of others while our struggle is evident for others to see.**

Christ saw the weaknesses of his disciples and urged them to pray so they would not fall into temptation. Jesus knew he was going to face betrayal, abandonment, and death but his concern was about the weaknesses of those he loved, and his prayer of intercession continued all the way to the cross, *"Father forgive them, for they do not know what they are doing."* **Luke 23:34 NIV**

Is anyone in your life in trouble or just causing trouble? Will you stay awake or wake up early and follow Christ in the garden or follow him to the cross? When we pray for others who are in trouble, we enter the prayer room of Christ. **Hebrews 7:24-25 NIV** - ... *"but because Jesus lives forever, he has a permanent priesthood. Therefore, he is able to save completely those who come to God through him, because he always lives to intercede for them." This* is an unselfish act of sowing a seed into someone's life whether you know or like them. When God places someone's trouble in your path, his unconditional love should motivate you to pray for them. God's love, compassion, forgiveness, is a part of God's character that is working in you to bring forth His power, even when it's inconvenient. Can He trust you with the trouble?

PRAY WITH ME

Father, Iam so grateful that You are aware of the unknown and can handle what I can't. Trouble gives little warning, but nothing catches You by surprise. Your plan for the cross and grave was for my benefit. Christ endured it all while praying for those who caused Him pain. What an unselfish sacrifice!

Help me to see You during trying times so I can endure and pray for someone else besides myself. Today, I announce that Iam presenting my life to You. **Romans 12:1 NIV-** *"Therefore, I urge you, brothers and sisters, in view of God's mercy, to offer your bodies as a living sacrifice, holy and pleasing to God—this is your true and proper worship."*

I refuse to bleed out with my feelings after You bled out for my righteousness. Lord, you called your work finished as you hung on the cross that I may live an abundant life and bring honor to your name. **John 19:30 NIV** – *"When he had received the drink, Jesus said, "It is finished." With that, he bowed his head and gave up his spirit."* As a living sacrifie, I will bear my cross in the prayer room to bring honor to Your name on behalf of someone else's life. **Teach me to pray, and to hear truth that will affect others to be free in Christ.** Help me to be at peace like You were and honor You with the sacrifice of intercession for someone in need.

REFLECTIONS

In your search for truth, what have you discovered about God and yourself? Write down your thoughts as you read or pray.

_____

_____

_____

_____

_____

_____

_____

_____

_____

_____

_____

_____

_____

_____

_____

_____

_____

DAY 25

For it is we who are the circumcision, we who serve God by his Spirit, who boast in Christ Jesus, and who put no confidence in the flesh—

Philippians 3:3 NIV

STRONG, BUT WEAK

Paul mentions his inheritance and being circumcised, as well as his lineage from the 12 tribes, but his boasting would only come from the point of having a relationship with Christ, while the other values in his life became secondary.

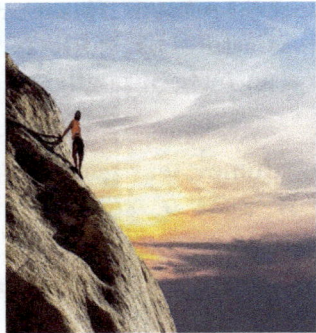

There was a time I was like Peter, I thought I could withstand temptation or the trickery schemes of darkness with unshaken faith. Now it makes sense that the Lord's Prayer includes in, Matthew 6:13 NIV *"And lead us not into temptation, but deliver us from the evil one"* … The word also informs us in **1Corinthians 10:13 NIV**- *No temptation has overtaken you except what is common to mankind. And God is faithful; he will not let you be tempted beyond what you can bear. But when you are tempted, he will also provide a way out so that you can endure it.*

God's word tells us that "for all have sinned and fallen short of the glory of God," … - **Romans 3:23**, but the word also says; *"I can do all things through Christ who strengthens me."* - **Philippians 4:13 NKJV** Therefore, when we surrender to God's will and way of doing things, the Spirit of God stands in our place of weakness that is within our sinful nature. Our level of surrender determines the probability of this happening, but our inability to understand the truth is often the reason for the delay. Remember, in **John 14:6 NIV** – *"Jesus answered, "I am the way and the **truth** and the life. No one comes to the Father except through me."* If we know Him, rather than know of Him and He knows us, we have truth and all the other treasures that come with Him.

As we seek to know and walk in God's Word, we develop confidence in our relationship with God. **Understanding the word should come from what the writer meant, rather than a person's personal interpretation. His** power moves with His word creating room for His glory. Now what was once weak is strong because His strength will always glorify Himself.

Are you plugged into the right source? No more running on fumes, let's get ready to be charged! But He said to me, *"My grace is sufficient for you, for my power is made perfect in weakness," therefore I will boast all the more gladly about my weaknesses, so that Christ's power may rest on me"*- **2Corinthians 12:9 NIV With** that being said, a believer must remember that God's grace answers in our "just in case" moments like just in case I fall; or I don't know what to do; just in case I find myself weak or incapable.

His sufficient grace has power and the ability to provide strength when we admit we need help. It is already determined that with God all things are possible. It's just a matter of how long it takes us to surrender.

PRAY WITH ME

Father, it has taken me some time to realize how weak I am, but you have waited patiently and protected me, even from myself. Thank you. I did not understand my weaknesses until I identified that what I had was not enough. Your grace has stepped in on many occasions, sparing my life from shame.

I welcome You into my space and every place of weakness, which should just about cover it all. You are my portion; my help and I am so glad You had me on Your mind with a plan when I had nothing.

Help me to trust you with this gift of life. Now my intentional focus will produce Your intended purpose. **Jeremiah 29:11-13 NIV** – *"For I know the plans I have for you," declares the Lord, "plans to prosper you and not to harm you, plans to give you hope and a future. Then you will call on me and come and pray to me, and I will listen to you. You will seek me and find me when you seek me with all your heart.* You promised I would find You when my whole heart was focused on You; therefore, Lord, satisfy my search and my response will bring much glory to Your name.

REFLECTIONS

In your search for truth, what have you discovered about God and yourself? Write down your thoughts as you read or pray.

_____

_____

_____

_____

_____

_____

_____

_____

_____

_____

_____

_____

_____

_____

_____

_____

_____

_____

DAY 26

> *"Be strong and courageous. Do not be afraid or discouraged because of the king of Assyria and the vast army with him, for here is a greater power with us than with him. With him is only the arm of flesh, but with us is the Lord our God to help us and to fight our battles."*

2 Chronicles 32:7 NIV

THE EQUATION OF VICTORY

Judah's walls were torn down and Hezekiah began the process of rebuilding them by gathering the people. He instructed the people to block the streams of water coming from their enemies to stop supplying them with water. Towers were built on top of the broken walls and the outer walls. Much work was put into this task and the people gained strength because they believed in their leader's message. In the end, victory was fully won when Hezekiah and the Prophet Isaiah prayed. **2 Chronicles 32:20** - *King Hezekiah and the prophet Isaiah son of Amoz cried out in prayer to heaven about this.*

In conclusion Faith, Works, and Prayer produce total victory for God's people and His glory. It's an absolute formula with no substitutes or compromises. Identify if something is missing from your equation and take hold of the missing part, then trust God for the results. Let's get started!

PRAY WITH ME

Father, thank you for awakening your truths in me today. Your presence is filled with greatness because you are a mighty fortress! Surround me with all Your glory that I may see the smallness of my enemies. The devices used to exploit my past failures will not delay my destiny. Your greatness is magnified in my eyes and my faith looks up to You in high places. No weapon formed against me shall prosper. I will not grow tired of doing what You declared good. Father, your divine protection is as present as you are. Help me to keep the formula of victory hidden in my heart as I work with others and to know that my labor is not in vain. I stand in agreement with Your righteous will to bring honor to your name and for your kingdom's sake.

REFLECTIONS

In your search for truth, what have you discovered about God and yourself? Write down your thoughts as you read or pray.

_____

_____

_____

_____

_____

_____

_____

_____

_____

_____

_____

_____

_____

_____

_____

DAY 27

The sacrifices of God are a broken spirit; a broken and contrite heart, Oh God, you will not despise.

Psalm 51:17 ESV

BROKEN

The Psalm of David in its entirety is a cry to the Lord for his mercy because he committed the sins of adultery and murder. He knew within his heart he had sinned against God, even though others had suffered from his actions. He made no excuses and admitted to disobeying a Holy God to satisfy his desires.

Growing up, we were often forced to apologize when we did something wrong, and we cooperated so we could continue playing or enjoying whatever activity was at hand. However, this plea for forgiveness was more than being sorry for getting caught, or sorry for the pain of his actions. He is filled with sorrow for his choice of behavior because it has interfered with his relationship with God and destroyed his fellowship with the Lord.

God does not treat men like broken glass to be thrown away or deemed worthless. Brokenness is usually caused by some type of impact from outside sources or too much pressure from the inside. In contrast, the Lord wants what is broken, what appears unusable, weak, or frail. The larger the cracks, the more space there is for God and His glory. Isn't it amazing that God who is omnipresent (everywhere at the same time) created man and then waits for him to invite Him in? God will take up as much room as we give Him. **Identifying the impact that caused the brokenness will help us to gain wisdom but yielding to God will give us greater victory.**

PRAY WITH ME

My God, in you I find strength to go on! I spent so much time blaming others for my problems that I prolonged the issue by trying to fix matters on my own. **Forgive me for taking so long to realize that "broken can't fix broken."** You are my creator, healer, and deliverer. There is no one like you and there will never be.

If man-made cleaners can accept dirty clothing and we willingly pay for cleaning services, then I will humble myself and bring my brokenness to a loving Father who will freely cleanse me from all unrighteousness. As I bow before your mercy seat, I trust in your faithfulness. My brokenness is laid at your altar and my heart seeks you for wisdom to stand in challenges, but this time I'm asking You to lead the way. There is a cry in my heart that tells me You are right and that I am ready to follow Your plans, Your way.

REFLECTIONS

<u>In your search for truth, what have you discovered about God and yourself? Write down your thoughts as you read or pray.</u>

_____

_____

_____

_____

_____

_____

_____

_____

_____

_____

_____

_____

_____

_____

DAY 28

Simon Peter answered, "You are the Messiah, the son of the living God." Jesus replied, "Blessed are you, Simon, son of Jonah, for this was not revealed to you by flesh and blood, but by my Father in heaven. And I tell you that you are Peter, and on this rock, I will build my church, and the gates of Hades will not overcome it. "I will give you the keys of the kingdom of heaven; whatever you bind on earth will be bound in heaven, and whatever you loose on earth will be loosed in heaven.

Matthew 16:16-17, 19 NIV

DID YOU PACK THE KEYS?

There has been a great deal of misinterpretation and misuse of the above scriptures. Christ asked Peter an insightful question that every believer must answer. "Who do you say I am?" The knowledge and understanding of who Jesus Christ is as the Messiah, the son of the living God, is "key." It is the solid foundation that the church (the body of Christ) was built on. In response, Jesus mounted a strong defense against the strategies of hell and His authority is passed on to those who follow him.

In the process of traveling, we may pack very few items or too much. We may end up leaving behind items we need or bringing unnecessary items. The most needed items for the journey are not discovered missing until we unpack what we're carrying or have a need for them.

Christ challenged Peter to unpack his thoughts and beliefs about who He was to him. After Peter's accurate response concerning the identity of Christ, Jesus confirmed Peter didn't get that information from man and offered him the keys to the kingdom of heaven.

Did you ever wonder, with all the time Peter spent with Jesus that it wasn't until he declared Him to be the Messiah that he was offered keys to God's kingdom? This moment of revelation brought forth a transformation that even changed Peter's name from Simon, son of Jonah. The changing of a person's name often means a change in character. Just in time, right before Peter fearfully denied knowing Christ. Thank God, the plans of God will not be changed by our weaknesses.

To acknowledge Christ's identity and to hear from heaven is evident that God is willing to reveal Himself to us although He is aware of our frailty. Jesus placed authority in frail hands like Peter because He was confident of His work in Peter just like He is of us who believe and follow Christ.

The use of this authority continues with believers who acknowledge Christ and are committed to God's will. In this instance, keys are used to open and lock doors, which is in line with the kingdom's purpose, rather than our own. It requires substantial responsibility but not without help. We are never alone. God has given us the Holy Spirit to lead and empower us with authority based on His word. **John 14:26 NIV** – *"But the Advocate, the Holy Spirit, whom the Father will send in my name, will teach you all things and will remind you of everything I have said to you."*

Believers in Christ are entrusted with awesome power and authority! It is given for God's people to stand in agreement with the heavens against what He forbids and to call forth or invite what He wants. This requires a faithful allegiance to truth and confidence that heaven will back you up! However, the question remains "What are you packing, and are you willing to get close enough to Christ to know how to use what He's willing to give you?" **Luke 10:19-20 NIV** – *"I have given you authority to trample on snakes and scorpions and to overcome all the power of the enemy; nothing will harm you. However, do not rejoice that the spirits submit to you, but rejoice that your names are written in heaven."*

PRAY WITH ME

Father, so many people have walked with you and still didn't know who you were. I understand that many followed you, but their hearts were far from You, and that others had a pretense of godliness, but would deny its power found in **Mark 7:6** and **2 Timothy 3:5**. Help me to see that knowing You is more than quoting scriptures, but embracing Your Lordship, love, and holiness.

Your authority is honored when I obey, and it makes room for You to show forth Your power and authority in my life. Thank you for opening my eyes to see and my ears to hear as the Spirit of God leads, empowers me, and keeps me. Jesus, you are my source. Let Your ways be clear to me, and I will know the truth. **John 14:6 NIV** – *"Jesus said, "I am the way, and the truth and the life. No one comes to the Father except through me."* As I embrace Christ, I have access to the Father, and while you call me friend, I call you Lord.

I am your servant and You have given me access to the king's quarters. As I pursue the Lord, I will discover the greatness and love of the Lord.

Oh, how majestic is Your name in all the earth! Even behind closed doors and after I say "Amen," my heart bows in reverence. You reign Lord! You are my guide throughout this journey, and in my weariness, allow me to soar like an eagle. **Isaiah 40:31 NIV**- *"but those who hope in the Lord will renew their strength. They will soar on wings like eagles; they will run* *and not grow weary; they will walk and not faint."* My faith thanks You in advance because I know of Your faithfulness.

REFLECTIONS

In your search for truth, what have you discovered about God and yourself? Write down your thoughts as you read or pray.

_____

_____

_____

_____

_____

_____

_____

_____

_____

_____

_____

_____

_____

_____

_____

_____

DAY 29

So he did what the Lord had told him. He went to the Kerith Ravine, east of the Jordan, and stayed there. The ravens brought him bread and meat in the morning and bread and meat in the evening, and he drank from the brook. Sometime later the brook dried up because there had been no rain in the land. Then the word of the Lord came to him; "Go at once to Zarephath in the region of Sidon and stay there. I have directed a widow there to supply you with food."

1 Kings 17:5-7, 9 NIV

GOD WILL PROVIDE

The word of God describes the journey of Elijah and God's sovereignty to use anything he chooses. God spoke and Elijah moved as instructed. God used ravens, which are not clean birds, but their condition did not limit God's ability or hinder His plans. Once the brook dried up the circumstances confirmed God's plan and that Elijah needed to hear God's voice again. **Knowing the voice of the Lord and His way will leave room for unusual provisions.**

One day while I was sick, I visited the doctor. I had a terrible cough, a fever, and was very weak. While waiting to see the doctor, I began to pray asking God to heal me. Soon after, an elderly lady came into the waiting room, sat down across from me and offered to pray for me. Her prayer was short and simple but full of faith.

99

When the doctor called me in, I tried to explain how I felt earlier and my experience with the lady, but he just stared at me. To our surprise, I was no longer coughing or running a fever. For a moment I was puzzled and questioned "Who was that, and what just happened?" When I left the office, I couldn't find her, but I was certain I was healed.

The unusual blessings of God are still available to those who believe, and God is still using whatever or whoever He chooses. Will you trust Him against the odds or for the unusual? Pay attention when He speaks through circumstances like a dry brook, especially during times of thirst. The dry brook was just an alarm for Elijah to get up because God had prepared a downpour of rain for his next encounter. Change is challenging, but the creator of the brook always has another way, even in the desert. He will provide.

PRAY WITH ME

My God, my Father, if you can create something out of nothing, you can certainly use anything! The world was framed by Your words that will never cease to exist. **Hebrews 11:3 NIV** – *"By faith we understand that the universe was formed at God's command, so that what is seen was not made out of what was visible."*

I declare that my trust is not in tangible things, for they will all fade away. I will not be shaken by a dried-up brook because You have prepared a table before me in the presence of my enemies. - **Psalms 23:5**

The weakness of this world or my body does not limit Your capacity to do amazing things! When I reach a dry brook, Lord, you are with me for the journey. I will thirst for Your righteousness and prepare for unusual blessings that speak of Your sovereignty and grace. These are the places and times that no one can take credit for. Help me to understand Your ways and keep me close enough to hear the

100

echoes of Your written word. There is more to see and know. My hunger and thirst for Your righteousness will fill my needs and I will be satisfied with You. **Matthew 5:6 NIV** – *"Blessed are those who hunger and thirst for righteousness, for they will be filled."* In this I find victory! Thank you.

REFLECTIONS

<u>In your search for truth, what have you discovered about God and yourself? Write down your thoughts as you read or pray.</u>

_____

_____

_____

_____

_____

_____

_____

_____

_____

_____

_____

_____

DAY 30

Isn't this the carpenter? Isn't this Mary's son and the brother of James, Joseph, Judas, and Simon? Aren't his sisters here with us?" And they took offense at him. Jesus said to them, "A prophet is not without honor except in his own town, among his relatives and in his own home." He could not do any miracles there, except lay his hands on a few sick people and heal them. He was amazed at their lack of faith.

Mark 6:3-6 NIV

THE CLASH OF UNBELIEF AND FAITH

People often find it difficult to accept a person's growth in Christ when growing up around family members and neighbors. The age of a person is not always an issue of acceptance. However, common mistakes made at an early age or before knowing the truth can make it difficult to accept who the individual has become.

These people were very familiar with Jesus and aware of his background, which made it too common for them to believe he was a prophet of God. The rejection of His identity, other than knowing His family fought against the faith needed to please God.

Witnessing or giving godly counsel to worldly friends or family can be challenging. The challenge is when people reject the person you have become because they won't let go of who you were. Some people may not have known you at a young age but knew you before your life was committed to

Christ. **It is difficult to understand the process of true transformation unless it is experienced.** Christ was amazed at their unbelief, but He moved on to others who were willing to embrace Him, the truth, and the power of God.

Don't stress, it may not be time yet, but the opportunity is there to do like Jesus did. Pray for a few sick people, witness God's grace, and see the glory of the Lord come to pass as you faithfully wait. Living God's way will impact a change in family and friends quicker than trying to tell them.

PRAY WITH ME

Father, my faith welcomes all of who you are and the miracles that come with you. My heart and eyes are eagerly awaiting the glory you will bring to my life today.

In every aspect of my life, your capacity far exceeds my request, and Your response is more than enough. **John 10:10 NIV –** *"The thief comes only to steal and kill and destroy; I came so that they would have life and have it abundantly."*

Give me wisdom to learn from Your experience with family and childhood friends. Lord, you considered your purpose to be more meaningful than their rejection. It may have hindered their blessing, but it never stopped You. Sometimes being up close can cause others to lose sight of what God wants to do in their life.

Continuing to trust in the love You freely gave, I understand that every rejection is not necessarily fatal, but merely a roadblock or a "not yet." I will not quit because there's always more to do for Your kingdom. Help me to be prepared for the unknown who may cross my path, and the people I least expect while I wait patiently for my loved ones. Thank you for counting me as one of Your loved ones when I didn't understand who You were. Through your grace I continue to see with understanding. **Ephesians 1:18 NKJV –**

"the eyes of your] understanding being enlightened; that you may know what is the hope of His calling, what are the riches of the glory of His inheritance in the saints." ...

REFLECTIONS

<u>In your search for truth, what have you discovered about God and yourself? Write down your thoughts as you read and pray.</u>

_____

_____

_____

_____

_____

_____

_____

_____

_____

_____

_____

_____

_____

DAY 31

His brothers then came and threw themselves down before him. "We are your slaves," they said. But Joseph said to them, "Don't be afraid, Am I in the place of God? You intended to harm me, but God intended it for good to accomplish what is now being done, the saving of many lives.

Genesis 50:18 NIV

CHANGING MY STORY!

Joseph's story of betrayal by his family, sold into slavery, lied on, and put in prison sounds like an awful life. However, God had a plan that would change his story. Transitioning to a changed life is incredibly challenging but responding to cruel treatment in a godly manner requires faith in God. Of course, it is not easy, but God's love is a life-changer and will help. The test of trust and one's character can often shine a light on where there is a lack of trust, or the need to make better choices. There is no magic in this process. The winds of change blow against our desires and direction; however, when surrender is seated in the heart of a believer God is always ready to lead.

Joseph transitioned from prison to power, from betrayal to becoming a beneficiary! And he blessed those who tried to hurt him because he realized their intentions were no match for God's ultimate plan to change his story. See, changing your story always includes someone else's story too. His story was so much more than his experience.

105

When the winds of change suddenly blow, things can get out of order, feelings get hurt, and nothing makes sense. **Knowing and trusting that God sees all will keep you focused until He is ready for you to soar for His glory.**

Trusting Him for the outcome is like wearing an oxygen mask on the plane. When turbulence strikes, hold on and don't panic. Trust God! He is a story changer

PRAY WITH ME

Father, thank you for the breath of life. When life changes, you never will. Breathe on me and restore me to the soundness of Your ways. Help me catch Your breath that refreshes and keeps me focused! You are my portion and my shelter in the storms of life. **Hebrews 13:6 NIV** – *"So we say with confidence, "The Lord is my helper; I will not be afraid. What can mere mortals do to me?"*

Yes, in every season You are there! If it were not so I would have been devoured. You are capable of handling me and my foes. Cause me to soar while I obey your will for the sake of Your kingdom and save my enemies so that Your name is glorified. The power of Your love makes all the difference.

You have demonstrated the integrity of your heart. Please help me to trust You when your plans are unknown to me. Your word says in **Jeremiah 29:12-13 NIV** – *"Then you will call on me and come and pray to me, and I will listen to you. You will seek me and find me when you seek me with all your heart."* Yes, the wonders of Your ways will be revealed!

While Your rewards are costly, they are worth it. I intend to be diligent in this endeavor because You are worthy. **Hebrews 11:6 NIV** – *"And without faith it is impossible to please God, because anyone who comes to him must believe that he exists and that he rewards those who earnestly seek him."*

Breathe on me again, and awaken me from any comas caused by fatalities, for these things are only for a moment. Nothing is comparable to what you have planned for those who love you. Thank you, Lord! Preparing for the flight and ready to go.

REFLECTIONS

<u>In your search for truth, what have you discovered about God and yourself? Write down your thoughts as you read or pray.</u>

_____

_____

_____

_____

_____

_____

_____

_____

_____

_____

_____

_____

_____

ACKNOWLEDGMENTS

This being my first book, but certainly not my last, I must take a moment to acknowledge God's grace to do this and contributions that enhanced this endeavor. Thanks to my husband, Pastor Craig Harrison, I received incredible support, encouragement, and love in completing this project. Thank you for your love and patience that enriches every area of my life.

TIWC family, knowing you are supporting this endeavor is always a blessing.

My appreciation continues to grow for Apostle Carlos L. Malone Sr., Lead Servant, The Bethel Church, for his support and words of encouragement.

My gratitude to Shawn McCulloch for supporting my vision with this book and pushing it forward with accountability.

Much gratitude to Abigail Couzens, PostureMe, L.L.C., who pushed me through this project with her words of affirmation and her demonstration as an entrepreneur.

www.ingramcontent.com/pod-product-compliance
Lightning Source LLC
LaVergne TN
LVHW022325080426
835508LV00013BA/1318

* 9 7 9 8 9 8 7 4 2 0 5 0 8 *